WHAT ARE TRAITS?

by Emily Sohn

PEBBLE
a capstone imprint

Pebble Explore is published by Pebble, an imprint of Capstone.
1710 Roe Crest Drive
North Mankato, Minnesota 56003
www.capstonepub.com

Library of Congress Cataloging-in-Publication Data
Names: Sohn, Emily, author.
Title: What are traits? / Emily Sohn.
Description: North Mankato, Minnesota : Pebble, [2022] | Series: Science inquiry | Includes bibliographical references and index. | Audience: Ages 5-8 | Audience: Grades 2-3 | Summary: "Some dogs are black. Other dogs are brown. Some plants have purple flowers and others have white flowers. Living things have different traits that they pass onto their offspring. Let's investigate traits to learn more!"— Provided by publisher.
Identifiers: LCCN 2021002770 (print) | LCCN 2021002771 (ebook) | ISBN 9781977131423 (hardcover) | ISBN 9781977132598 (paperback) | ISBN 9781977155276 (pdf) | ISBN 9781977156891 (kindle edition)
Subjects: LCSH: Genetics—Juvenile literature. | Heredity—Juvenile literature.
Classification: LCC QH437.5 .S65 2022 (print) | LCC QH437.5 (ebook) | DDC 576.5—dc23
LC record available at https://lccn.loc.gov/2021002770
LC ebook record available at https://lccn.loc.gov/2021002771

Image Credits
iStockphoto: blackCAT, 28, kali9, 23, maccj, 25; Shutterstock: Africa Studio, 21, alexei_tm, 27 (bottom), AndriyShevchuk, 5, Anke van Wyk, 19, artellia, 17, eltoro69, 12, gengirl, 15, KELENY, 9 (top), Lopolo, 1, 27 (t), Lunja, 20, Monkey Business Images, 29, Nick Chase 68, 9 (b), PCHT cover, Picmin, 10, 11, Susan Schmitz, 7, Tom Wang, 13, WildMedia, 14

Artistic elements: Shutterstock/balabolka

Editorial Credits
Editor: Erika L. Shores; Designer: Dina Her; Media Researcher: Kelly Garvin; Production Specialist: Tori Abraham

TABLE OF CONTENTS

Words in **bold** are in the glossary.

A TRAIT INVESTIGATION

Look in the mirror. What do you see? Notice the color of your eyes, hair, and skin. Look at the shape of your nose and ears. You probably look like your family members. But there are differences too.

Each detail about you is called a trait. Animals and plants have traits too. Traits describe how living things look. They also describe how living things act, or behave.

Let's do an investigation to learn more about traits. Look at each dog on page 7. Notice the color of its fur. Does it have pointy ears or floppy ears? What about the shape of its nose? List as many traits as you can.

Now compare the dogs. Pick two. Write a list of ways they are similar. Next, write some ways they are different.

The puppies are brothers and sisters. They all have the same parents. But they look different from each other.

Choose one of the puppies. Look at the parents. How is the puppy like its mother? How is it like its father? How is it like each of its siblings?

Draw another puppy. Make it look different from its siblings. But give it traits in common with its mother and father.

father

mother

9

HOW DO PLANTS PASS ALONG TRAITS?

Plants have parents too. Let's look at pea plants. Some are tall. Some are short. Flowers can be white or purple. Pods can be green or yellow. Peas can be wrinkled or smooth.

When plants **reproduce**, they make new plants. The new plants are their **offspring**. Just like in animals, they are what is called a new **generation**. Look at each photo. What do you think the plants' offspring will look like?

Pea plants make new pea plants. Oak trees make new oak trees. Raspberry bushes make new raspberry bushes. **Heredity** explains how traits get passed from parents to offspring. This kind of trait is called an **inherited** trait.

young oak tree

In both plants and animals, offspring will look like their parents. But they won't look exactly the same. Pea plants with white flowers can have offspring with purple flowers. Tall parents can have short offspring.

Heredity happens in animal **species** too. A single type of living thing is called a species. Bears have bear cubs, not grasshoppers. Cats give birth to kittens, not elephants.

There will be small changes with every generation. But each species makes more of the same species.

ARE ALL TRAITS INHERITED?

Look at the puppies on page 7. They get their colors, body shapes, and ear sizes from their parents. Traits move from parent to offspring in tiny units called **genes.** We can't see genes. But they explain much of how plants and animals look.

A mom's genes and a dad's genes mix, or combine, in many ways. That's why two puppies in a litter might look so different. It is also why pea plants can look different from their parents.

PARENT 1		PARENT 2			EYE COLOR of the BABY		
👁	+	👁	=		👁	👁	👁
					75%	18.75%	6.25%
👁	+	👁	=		👁	👁	👁
					50%	37.5%	12.5%
👁	+	👁	=		👁	👁	👁
					50%	0%	50%
👁	+	👁	=		👁	👁	👁
					<1%	75%	25%
👁	+	👁	=		👁	👁	👁
					0%	50%	50%
👁	+	👁	=		👁	👁	👁
					0%	1%	99%

A child gets their eye color from their parents' genes. This chart shows which color a child might have depending on their parents' eye color.

Two puppies get in a fight. They bite and scratch. One clips the other's ear. One scratches the other's leg. Both puppies are OK, but they look a little different now.

Scars are acquired traits. These traits don't come from a dog's parents. And they won't get passed on to the dog's puppies.

DO TRAITS ONLY DESCRIBE LOOKS?

You throw a ball. Two puppies race for it. Traits describe more than just looks. They also include behaviors like running, jumping, and barking.

Personality is another kind of behavior that is inherited. Some dogs are shy. Some are friendly. Some are calm. Their genes may help explain many of these traits.

One dog gets to the ball first.
It brings the ball back to you.
You pet the pup and give it a treat.

Playing fetch is a learned trait. Dogs
may also learn not to bark or pee in the
house. They can learn which beds they
can sleep on. Dogs don't know how
people want them to act when they
are born. We have to teach them.

HOW DO HEREDITY AND LEARNING WORK TOGETHER?

Genes and learning combine to make us how we are. People can swim. Our genes give us the ability to do it. But some people have long arms. It might be easier for them to swim fast. Still, anyone can learn to swim faster by practicing more. Other learned traits include talking, writing, and reading.

Genes are sometimes called **nature**. They give us the abilities we are born with. **Nurture** describes the experiences that shape us.

Twins show how nature and nurture work together. Identical twins have the same genes. They look alike. But they are unique.

If one twin meets a mean dog that barks loudly, she might become afraid of dogs. If the other twin meets a nice dog, she might learn to love dogs. The twins have the same genes. But they have different feelings about dogs.

WHAT CAN YOU LEARN FROM YOUR TRAITS?

Look in the mirror again. Draw a picture of yourself. Label the traits that you inherited. This may include your eye color and ear size. Now label the traits you have acquired. You could draw scars, pierced ears, or short or long hair.

Think about your behaviors. Write a list of what you like to do and how you act. Are you quiet or chatty? Daring or careful? Silly or serious? Which of these traits have you learned? Which do you think are in your genes?

Plants, animals, and people all have traits. These details help make the world an interesting place.

GLOSSARY

gene (JEEN)—a part of every cell that carries physical and behavioral characteristics an offspring inherits from its parents

generation (jen-uh-RAY-shuhn)—all the members of a group of people or creatures born around the same time

heredity (huh-RED-i-tee)—the process through which characteristics are passed from parents to offspring

inherit (in-HER-it)—to receive something from a parent, such as looks, habits, or skills

nature (NAY-cher)—all the genes that affect how a person or animal looks and acts

nurture (NUR-cher)—the way that a person or an animal was raised

offspring (OF-spring)—the young of a person, animal, or plant

reproduce (ree-pruh-DOOSE)—to make offspring

species (SPEE-sheez)—a group of animals or plants with common characteristics or features

READ MORE

Anders, Mason. *Heredity*. North Mankato, MN: Capstone Press, 2018.

Gaertner, Meg. *Puppies*. Lake Elmo, MN: Focus Readers, 2020.

Kalman, Bobbie. *What Kind of Animal Is It?* New York: Crabtree Publishing Company, 2018.

INTERNET SITES

Variation of Traits
generationgenius.com/videolessons/variation-of-traits-video-for-kids/

What Is a Gene?
kidshealth.org/en/kids/what-is-gene.html

INDEX